Babushka

by Ruth Kenward

for Pat

Starshine Music

www.starshine.co.uk

Brown Cottage, Glynleigh Road, Hankham, East Sussex, England, BN24 5BJ.
Tel: +44 (0)1323 764334 Fax: +44 (0)1323 767145 E-mail: info@starshine.co.uk

With gratitude for the contribution made by Maggie Hughes.

Grateful acknowledgement is due to the following schools for conducting trials of 'Babushka':
Church Lane Primary School & Nursery, Sleaford, Lincs
Margaret Stancomb Inf/Nurs School, Trowbridge, Wilts
Lancashire Performing Arts Centre, Lancashire
Parkland Junior School, Eastbourne, East Sussex
Great Ballard School, Eartham, West Sussex

ISBN Nos.
Musical Book: 978-1-905591-28-2
Multimedia pack: 987-1-905591-29-9

Cover illustration by Sophie Fatus

Director's Notes

CAST LIST

(In order of appearance)

Narrators	Scripted for two narrators, but may be shared between more.	
Babushka	Large speaking part. SOLO singer required.	
Fly, Mouse, Spider	Small speaking parts. Could be two of each,	Scene 1
Star	Non-speaking part,	Scene 1
Cloud	Non-speaking part,	Scene 1
Angel	Small speaking part. SOLO/GROUP singer required,	
Kings 1,2,3	Medium speaking part. TRIO singers required,	
Camels 1,2,3	Small speaking part. TRIO singers required,	
Angels	Non-speaking parts, as many as required,	Scenes 1, 2, 3
Cattle/Donkeys/Sheep	As many as required. Group singing,	
Mother, Child	Small speaking parts,	Scene 2
Old Woman (or Man)	Small speaking part,	Scene 2
Shepherd Boy	Small speaking part,	Scene 2
Mary	Small speaking part. SOLO singer required,	Scene 3
Donkey	Small speaking part,	Scene 3
Joseph	Small speaking part,	Scene 3

PROPS

To be set before the play begins:

Chair (ideally a rocking chair) in which Babushka sleeps (to be taken off after Scene 1).
Cleaning equipment for Babushka: duster, polish, rubber gloves.
Candlesticks for Babushka to polish.
Star on stick to be held by 'Star' performer.
Basket for Babushka.
Placed in three different locations in Babushka's 'house': small rag doll, shawl, bottle.
Doll to be Baby Jesus in the crib scene.
Manger.

To be carried on by performers:

Broom for Babushka.
Walking stick for old woman.
'Glass' for Joseph.
Enormous hankie for Girl.
Lamb for Shepherd Boy.
Gold, frankincense and myrrh for camels.

STAGING SUGGESTIONS

Scenery is not essential, as most scenes can be suggested by the use of props.
If painted scenes on flats are to be used, they should be as follows:

Scene 1	Rustic kitchen scene – cooker, cupboard, window with cloud in view, allowing child to be seen behind it.
Scene 2	Outdoor scene, trees, flowers, etc.
Scene 3	Stable – traditional nativity backdrop.

If scenery changes are not possible, one side of the stage could be set as Babushka's house and the other side could be set as the stable.

NARRATIVE VERSION

A narrated version of the show can be found on page 59. It is written for four narrators, but this can be reduced or expanded as required.

Director's Overview

Scene 1 **Outside Babushka's House** (p. 7) *[Choreography p. 5/6]*

The villagers meet and greet each other. Babushka is too busy to dance.

DANCE	RUSSIAN VILLAGERS' DANCE	⊙ Track 1 / 14

Scene 2 **Inside Babushka's House** (p. 7)

Babushka's house is the cleanest in Russia. She shoos creatures away.

CHANT	YOU'LL NEVER FIND A MOUSE	⊙ Track 2 / 15

Babushka cleans so much because she is unhappy.

SONG	BABUSHKA (EMPTY HEART)	⊙ Track 3 / 16

Babushka is so busy cleaning that she doesn't notice a bright new star in the sky. An angel appears outside her window, telling her he brings good news. She won't let him in, she is too concerned about her clean floor. Soon after, she treats three kings and their camels in the same way.

SONG	WIPE YOUR FEET	⊙ Track 4 / 17

Babushka goes to sleep, tired after all the fuss. The angel returns and sings to her about the stable in which a baby has been born.

SONG	THERE'S A STABLE	⊙ Track 5 / 18

Babushka wakes when the star shines in through the window. She remembers what she heard while she was sleeping. She's disgusted at the thought of a new baby in a dirty old stable and sets off for Bethlehem with a basket of gifts and cleaning equipment.

INSTR.	BABUSHKA PACKS HER BASKET	⊙ Track 6 / 19
SONG	TO BETHLEHEM	⊙ Track 7 / 20

Scene 3 **Babushka's journey** (p. 12)

On her way, she meets a mother whose child is crying; she has lost her doll. Babushka gives her the rag doll, before continuing on her journey.

SONG	TO BETHLEHEM (REPRISE)	⊙ Track 8 / 21

Next, she meets an old woman who is tired and thirsty, and her legs are aching. Babushka gives the old woman the cordial to drink, and she immediately feels much better. Babushka continues on her journey.

SONG	TO BETHLEHEM (REPRISE)	⊙ Track 9 / 22

Then Babushka comes across a shepherd boy who is shivering with cold. She gives him the warm shawl. Then she realises that she has nothing left to give the baby. Sadly, she turns for home.

INSTR.	BABUSHKA TURNS BACK	⊙ Track 10 / 23

Scene 4 **In The Stable** (p. 15)

Mary calls her into the stable. Babushka is disgusted to see the dirty animals, but quickly forgets this when she sees the baby, and finds that the things she gave away have mysteriously arrived at the stable.

SONG	EVERYTHING YOU GIVE	⊙ Track 11 / 24
SONG	BABUSHKA (FULL HEART)	⊙ Track 12 / 25

The kings and camels arrive at the stable. Joseph welcomes them in. Babushka apologises for her rudeness to them. The kings give their gifts to the baby and – like Babushka – are filled with peace. Everyone dances.

SONG	MY FEET WANT TO DANCE	⊙ Track 13 / 26

Russian Villagers' Dance

Suggested Choreography

The dance shown overleaf may be performed by any number of dancers. For simplicity, the instructions refer to boy/girl partnerships, but this is not essential. The style of the dance requires a proud, upright body carriage with strong, positive steps and gestures. The music is composed in 2/4 time.

Explanation of Steps, Positions and Pathways

<u>Directions and Pathways</u>	Forward - F	Backwards - B
	Side right - R	Side left - L

<u>Spin</u>

In place step R and propel yourself round in a clockwise direction using the ball of L foot. Use the regular rhythmic beat in the music. Repeat 4 times.

<u>Heel Beats</u>

Extend Right heel diagonally to Forward Right and place on the floor, return to place.

Repeat with Left heel diagonally to Forward Left and return to place. 2 counts out and 2 counts to return.

<u>Creative Option</u>

Experienced and confident teachers / dancers may wish to work more freely and imaginatively with Section 2. Use basic steps of heel beats, spins, runs and stamps. Dancers' own variations of steps and gestures should be encouraged. In pairs develop a sequence using: unison, question and answer and travelling towards, away and around your partner. Use the same musical structure designated for Section 2.

<u>Tip</u>

An easy way for young dancers to achieve a Cossack dance effect is to have them sitting on a low bench or staging block and doing L / R kicks with Cossack arms. A group could be seated doing this during the repeat section, while others perform the full dance on the stage.

Russian Villagers' Dance

Suggested Choreography

SECTION	MUSIC	DANCE IDEA	MOVEMENT MATERIAL
Introduction	8 Bars	Villagers meet and greet in preparation for the dance	• Dancers walk purposefully on the beat (16 steps) to form two concentric circles, boys on the outside and girls on the inside, all facing the centre. Feet together, weight central, upright stance in place. • Boys: fists on hips, elbows out to the side. • Girls: hands on hips, elbows out to the side. 
Section 1: Circle Dance	16 Bars	Joyful, proud, unifying, social dance. Movement towards and away from the centre, then turning on the spot.	• 4 heel beats (R,L,R,L) Bars 1-4 • 3 walks Forwards, RLR stamp L Bars 5-6 • 3 walks Backwards, LRL stamp R Bars 7-8 • 4 heel beats (R,L,R,L) Bars 9-12 • Spin, arms in high V ←  Bars 13-14 • 3 stamps and hold facing partner (girls turn outwards to face boys) Bars 15-16
Section 2: Partner Dance	16 Bars	Partner dance. Question, answer and unison; vitality & display.	• Girl travels round boy, who stays in place: 8 running steps, kicking heels up behind, arms in Cossack position (R hand above L elbow, L hand below R elbow) ←  Bars 1-4 • Girl & boy spin using arms in high V, palms facing. Bars 5-6 • 3 stamps facing, hands/fists on hips Bars 7-8 • Repeat the sequence above commencing with boy travelling round girl, who stands in place. Bars 9-16
Transition	2 bar bridge to slow tempo	Return to starting positions	• Step back into two concentric circles, standing in place as at the beginning, feet together, hands/fists on hips facing the centre.
REPEAT			• Repeat the whole dance but commence Section 1 with a slow emphatic tempo to echo the pace and quality in the music.
ENDING			• Coming out of the final spin in the repeat of Section 2, all end facing centre, with an emphatic stamp, and arms stretched up into a high V, palms facing, all shouting 'Hoi!'

Please remember that all performances must be by prior arrangement with the Publishers from whom licences must be obtained.

Babushka

SCENE 1 Outside Babushka's House

[Enter VILLAGERS, meeting and greeting in a dance.]

RUSSIAN VILLAGERS' DANCE (⊙ Track 1 / 14)

SCENE 2 Inside Babushka's House

NARRATOR 1 — Long ago, in a Russian village, there lived a little old woman called Babushka. She was as round and kindly as a warm plum pudding.

[Enter BABUSHKA, sweeping and dusting.]

NARRATOR 2 — While everyone else was dancing, she would sweep, dust and polish from sunrise to starshine.

NARRATOR 1 — Her house was the cleanest in the whole of Russia.

BABUSHKA — (proudly) My house is the cleanest in the whole of Russia!

[MOUSE, SPIDER & FLY enter (or two of each). At the end of each verse, BABUSHKA chases them off with her broom.]

YOU'LL NEVER FIND A MOUSE (⊙ Track 2 / 15)

All *(reciting)*
YOU'LL NEVER FIND A MOUSE
IN BABUSHKA'S HOUSE.
IT'S FAR TOO CLEAN
FOR A MOUSE TO BE SEEN!
FAR TOO CLEAN
FOR A MOUSE TO BE SEEN!
BYE, BYE MOUSE!
BYE, BYE MOUSE!

← MOUSE tries to creep past BABUSHKA. On 'bye bye' he gets swept away. Goes to stand to one side, looking afraid.

YOU'LL NEVER FIND A SPIDER
SITTING DOWN BESIDE HER.
IT'S FAR TOO CLEAN
FOR A SPIDER TO BE SEEN!
FAR TOO CLEAN
FOR A SPIDER TO BE SEEN!

← SPIDER tries to creep past BABUSHKA. On 'bye, bye' he gets swept away. Goes to join MOUSE, looking afraid.

BYE, BYE SPIDER!
BYE, BYE SPIDER!

YOU'LL NEVER FIND A FLY
BUZZING, BUZZING BY.
IT'S FAR TOO CLEAN
FOR A FLY TO BE SEEN!
FAR TOO CLEAN
FOR A FLY TO BE SEEN!
BYE, BYE FLY!
BYE, BYE FLY!

← FLY tries to fly past BABUSHKA. On 'bye, bye' he gets swept away. Goes to join MOUSE & SPIDER, looking afraid.

YOU'LL NEVER FIND *(clap, clap)* *['sliced' as if a job is finished]*
A SPECK OF DUST. *(clap, clap)*
BABUSHKA CLEANS *(clap, clap)*
FROM DAWN 'TIL DUSK!

[BABUSHKA keeps cleaning, her back to SPIDER, MOUSE & FLY.]

FLY *(sadly, spreading arms)* Why does Babushka clean so much?

MOUSE *(sadly shaking head)* There are no crumbs for us to eat …

SPIDER *(crossly)* It's so clean and tidy, we've got nowhere to hide!

FLY/MOUSE/SPIDER *(very sadly)* She hates us!

ALL Ahh!

[BABUSHKA notices FLY, MOUSE & SPIDER again and chases them away with her broom.]

BABUSHKA Shoo! Shoo! You horrible dirty things!

[BABUSHKA moves around miming cleaning activities, and continues this throughout the following song, making her actions match the words. The CHORUS can mime the same activities.]

NARRATOR 1 Babushka kept busy all the time because she had an empty place in her heart.

NARRATOR 2 Poor Babushka. She was busy but she wasn't happy.

BABUSHKA (Empty Heart) **(⊙ Track 3 / 16)**

BABUSHKA. BABUSHKA.
SHE HIDES AN EMPTY PLACE IN HER HEART.

(Repeat)

SWEEPING, SWEEPING,
SWEEPING ALL DAY LONG.
SHE'S NO TIME TO STOP AND THINK,
SWEEPING ALL DAY LONG.

DUSTING, DUSTING,
DUSTING ALL DAY LONG.
SHE'S NO TIME TO STOP AND THINK,
DUSTING ALL DAY LONG.

WASHING, WASHING,
WASHING ALL DAY LONG.
SHE'S NO TIME TO STOP AND THINK,
WASHING ALL DAY LONG.

BUSY, BUSY,
BUSY ALL DAY LONG.
SHE'S NO TIME TO STOP AND THINK....
(SPOKEN) STOP, BABUSHKA!
IT'S ALREADY CLEAN.

BABUSHKA. BABUSHKA.
SHE HIDES AN EMPTY PLACE IN HER HEART.

[BABUSHKA sits in her chair and polishes candlesticks through the following narration.]

NARRATOR 1 — Poor Babushka had no friends. She was very lonely. All she did was clean her house.

NARRATOR 2 — One evening a bright new star shone through Babushka's window.

[STAR moves into position.]

NARRATOR 1 — She was polishing her candlesticks, when something made her look at the window. Look at the star, Babushka!

[BABUSHKA looks towards the window.]

ALL — Look, Babushka!

NARRATOR 2 — But she didn't notice the star. She was too busy noticing a dirty mark on the window pane.

[BABUSHKA starts to rise from her chair as she speaks ready to move towards the window.]

BABUSHKA — *(tutting)* How did that get there? What a disgrace!

[BABUSHKA takes a cloth, goes to the window and cleans it. STAR moves out of sight. ANGEL moves into view.]

BABUSHKA — *(stepping back to admire her work)* That's better – all clean. Now I can see out!

[BABUSHKA peers out of the window.]

NARRATOR 2 — It was too late for Babushka to see the star. It was hiding behind a cloud. But she saw something else instead – an angel!

ANGEL — Hello Babushka! I bring you good news!

ALL — Listen to the news, Babushka!

BABUSHKA — Humph! *(bossily, pointing at ANGEL's feet)* You'll have to wipe your feet if you want to come in!

[ANGEL looks very sad, wings droop, head hangs.]

NARRATOR 1 — Babushka wasn't bothered about the good news! That made the angel very sad, and he flew away.

ALL — Ahh.... poor angel.

[Exit ANGEL, flapping wings. BABUSHKA goes back to her chair and polishes. KINGS approach the door.]

NARRATOR 2 — Babushka wondered what the angel's news might have been. But it was too late to find out. Soon there was a knock at the door.

[Knocking sound.]

BABUSHKA — Who can that be?

[BABUSHKA mimes opening a door. Enter KINGS, to stand centrally and sing. BABUSHKA stands with her arms folded looking suspicious.]

<u>WIPE YOUR FEET</u> (⊙ Track 4 / 17)

Kings
WE ARE KINGS FROM AFAR
FOLLOWING THAT BRIGHT STAR,
WE'RE TAKING GIFTS TO A CHILD.
MAY WE REST FOR A WHILE?
MAY WE REST FOR A WHILE? PLEASE?

Babushka
(pointing at their feet)
WIPE YOUR FEET! WIPE YOUR FEET!
WIPE YOUR NASTY, DIRTY FEET!

All
WIPE YOUR FEET! WIPE YOUR FEET!
WIPE YOUR NASTY, DIRTY FEET!
WIPE YOUR FEET! *(shouted)*

Kings: *(spoken crossly)* Huh! She ought to be more polite! We're kings!

[KINGS fold arms, and get in a huddle, as if grumbling.]

Camels
WE ARE THE CAMEL TRAIN.
CARRYING KINGS IS A PAIN.
WE'RE TAKING GIFTS TO A CHILD.
MAY WE REST FOR A WHILE?
MAY WE REST FOR A WHILE? PLEASE?

Babushka
(pointing at their hooves)
WIPE YOUR HOOVES! WIPE YOUR HOOVES!
WIPE YOUR NASTY, DIRTY HOOVES!

All
WIPE YOUR HOOVES! WIPE YOUR HOOVES!
WIPE YOUR NASTY, DIRTY HOOVES!
WIPE YOUR HOOVES! *(shouted)*

BABUSHKA	*(waving them away)* You're too dirty! Shoo!
CAMEL	*(scared)* Ooh! She's bossier than my mum!
CAMELS	*(panicky)* Run away! Run away!
	[CAMELS run off.]
KING 1	*(in posh voice)* I say, chaps, where did our camels go?
KINGS 2 & 3	Oh no! Our camels have run away!
KING 1	Quick! After them!
	[KINGS run off.]
BABUSHKA	*(hands on hips)* I'm glad they've gone. They would have made such a mess!
	[BABUSHKA sits on her chair as NARRATOR speaks.]
NARRATOR 1	Babushka was tired after all that fuss, so she sat down for a rest. She thought about the kings and the camels, and the long journey they must have had.
BABUSHKA	I suppose they must have been very tired… *(tuts and shakes her head as if thinking about their long journey)*
NARRATOR 2	She felt sorry for the kings and the camels, but she couldn't have coped with all those dirty feet and hooves.
BABUSHKA	*(showing six fingers)* Six dirty feet! Tut, tut, tut! *(opening arms out)* And twelve dirty hooves! Tut, tut, tut!
NARRATOR 1	Babushka yawned, and very soon she fell asleep.
	[BABUSHKA yawns, stretches, then settles to sleep.]
NARRATOR 2	While she was sleeping the angel came back and sang a song about a baby being born.
	[If time for movement onto stage is needed, use the backing to play ANGELS, DONKEYS & SHEEP on, fading out when ready and re-starting the track.]

THERE'S A STABLE (⊙ Track 5 / 18)

Angel(s) THERE'S A STABLE FULL OF COBWEBS
SHABBY AND OLD,
AND IT'S DIRTY, VERY DUSTY,
GLOOMY AND COLD.

Angel(s) BUT TONIGHT THAT TATTY STABLE
IS BLAZING WITH LIGHT,
'COS A BABY'S BEEN BORN TONIGHT.

All THERE'S A STABLE FULL OF COBWEBS
SHABBY AND OLD,

AND IT'S DIRTY, VERY DUSTY,
GLOOMY AND COLD.
BUT TONIGHT THAT TATTY STABLE
IS BLAZING WITH LIGHT,
'COS A BABY'S BEEN BORN TONIGHT.

Cattle, Donkeys & Sheep IN THE STABLE THERE ARE CATTLE,
DONKEYS AND SHEEP,
AND THEIR EYES ARE SO WIDE OPEN,
THEY JUST CAN'T SLEEP.

All 'COS TONIGHT THAT TATTY STABLE
IS BLAZING WITH LIGHT,
'COS A BABY'S BEEN BORN TONIGHT.
YES, A BABY'S BEEN BORN TONIGHT.

[STAR moves into position during last line of song.]

NARRATOR 2 As the angel finished singing, the star peeped out from behind the cloud and shone in through the window.

NARRATOR 1 It woke Babushka up.

[BABUSHKA yawns and stretches.]

She remembered what she'd heard while she was sleeping.

BABUSHKA *(jumping up)* A brand new baby in a dirty old stable? *(hands on hips)* How disgusting!

NARRATOR 2 Babushka knew she had to do something to help this little baby. She felt so sorry for him, born in a scruffy stable.

BABUSHKA Poor baby! I must set off at once.

[BABUSHKA starts packing her basket, and keeps miming getting ready to go throughout the music.]

BABUSHKA PACKS HER BASKET (⊙ Track 6 / 19)

NARRATOR 1 *(speaking over the incidental music)* Babushka packed a basket with a little rag doll, a warm shawl and a bottle of ginger cordial for the grown-ups. She also packed some cleaning equipment.

[Chair is removed. Scenery may be changed, and ANGELS begin to spread out at the back of the performing area.]

SCENE 3 Babushka's Journey

NARRATOR 2 Outside the house the sky grew very bright as lots of angels crowded around. They watched over Babushka as she set out on her journey, but she didn't notice them.

[BABUSHKA stands with her basket over her arm to sing the

first verse, then sets off walking around as if on a journey, while the ANGELS & ALL OTHER PERFORMERS sing verse 2. A few ANGELS may follow BABUSHKA.]

TO BETHLEHEM (⊙ Track 7 / 20)

Babushka I MUST GO TO BETHLEHEM,
BETHLEHEM, BETHLEHEM.
WHEN I GET TO BETHLEHEM
I SHALL FIND THE BABY.

All SHE MUST GO TO BETHLEHEM,
BETHLEHEM, BETHLEHEM.
WHEN SHE GETS TO BETHLEHEM
SHE WILL FIND THE BABY,
SHE WILL FIND THE BABY.

MOTHER enters, holding the hand of CHILD, who is crying loudly.

BABUSHKA *(sympathetically)* Oh dear! What's the matter?

[CHILD gets out enormously big hankie from pocket, and blows nose very loudly.]

MOTHER We were running to see the new king and my little girl dropped her dolly.

CHILD *(wailing very sadly)* It fell out of my pocket... and it's gone!

BABUSHKA *(putting an arm around CHILD's shoulder)* Ahh... Poor you!

[If possible the CHILD should cry in an obviously exaggerated way until the audience laugh. BABUSHKA gets out the doll during the laughter and narration.]

NARRATOR 1 Babushka took the toy doll out of her basket and jiggled it to make it dance. The little girl stopped crying, smiled and pointed at the doll.

CHILD *(smiling cutely)* Look, mum! Isn't it sweet!

BABUSHKA Take it, with my love. It's good to see you smile.

CHILD *(with a delighted smile)* Thank you, Babushka!

MOTHER You are so kind! Thank you for cheering her up.

CHILD Goodbye! We're off to see the new king!

[MOTHER & CHILD exit, waving, going to join nativity group. BABUSHKA waves them off. CHILD must remember to put the doll in the crib.]

BABUSHKA *(to audience, finger on chin)* A new king? That's interesting. You don't get a new king every day...

NARRATOR 2 Babushka continued on her journey, wondering how the little girl knew her name. That was very strange.

[BABUSHKA walks around as if on a journey. A few ANGELS may follow her.]

<u>TO BETHLEHEM</u> (reprise) **(⊙ Track 8 / 21)**

All SHE MUST GO TO BETHLEHEM,
BETHLEHEM, BETHLEHEM.
WHEN SHE GETS TO BETHLEHEM
SHE WILL FIND THE BABY,
SHE WILL FIND THE BABY.

OLD WOMAN enters, bent over, hobbling with a stick and clutching her back.

BABUSHKA *(sympathetically)* Oh dear! What's the matter?

OLD WOMAN *(in a wobbly old voice)* I am going to see a new baby, but I can't go very fast. I'm tired and thirsty, and my legs ache so much.

NARRATOR 1 Babushka took the bottle of cordial out of her basket and gave it to the old woman.

BABUSHKA Take this with my love. It'll do you a power of good.

OLD WOMAN *(in a wobbly old voice)* Bless you, Babushka! You are very kind.

NARRATOR 1 The old woman took a big drink and all of a sudden she stood up straight with a big smile.

OLD WOMAN *(with a skip and a jump)* Hooray! I feel ten years younger! Now it'll be an easy journey to see the new baby! Goodbye!

[OLD WOMAN exits, waving, then goes to join nativity group. BABUSHKA waves her off. OLD WOMAN must remember to give the bottle of cordial to JOSEPH.]

BABUSHKA *(to audience, finger on chin)* A new baby? That's interesting! I'm going to see a new baby too!

NARRATOR 2 Babushka continued on her journey, wondering how the old woman knew her name. That was very strange.

[BABUSHKA walks around as if on a journey. A few ANGELS may follow her.]

<u>TO BETHLEHEM</u> (reprise) **(⊙ Track 9 / 22)**

All SHE MUST GO TO BETHLEHEM,
BETHLEHEM, BETHLEHEM.
WHEN SHE GETS TO BETHLEHEM
SHE WILL FIND THE BABY,
SHE WILL FIND THE BABY.

SHEPHERD BOY enters carrying a lamb, shivering and rubbing his arms

BABUSHKA *(sympathetically)* Oh dear! What's the matter?

SHEPHERD BOY *(shivering)* I'm so cold! I can't carry this lamb much further!

[BABUSHKA gets out the shawl during the narration.]

NARRATOR 1 — Babushka took the warm shawl out of her basket. She put the basket down, and wrapped the shawl around the shepherd boy's shoulders.

BABUSHKA — Take this with my love. It will keep you warm on your journey.

NARRATOR 2 — The shepherd boy stopped shivering and smiled at Babushka.

SHEPHERD BOY — Thank you, Babuhska! Now I must catch up with the other shepherds. We're going to see the new baby king! Goodbye!

[SHEPHERD BOY exits, waving, then goes to join nativity group. BABUSHKA waves him off. SHEPHERD BOY must put the shawl around the Jesus doll.]

BABUSHKA — *(to audience, finger on chin)* A new baby king? So we've had... *(counts with fingers)* a new baby, a new king, and a new baby king! *(shrugs)*

NARRATOR 1 — Then Babushka realised something else. The shepherd boy had known her name, just like the little girl and the old woman! This journey was getting stranger by the minute!

BABUSHKA — *(to audience)* This journey is getting stranger by the minute!

NARRATOR 1 — Babushka picked up her basket, and gave a little gasp.

BABUSHKA — *(gasps)* Oh no! *(very sadly)* I'm such a silly old woman! I've given all the presents away...

NARRATOR 2 — Sadly, Babushka turned back towards home. She didn't want to go and see the new baby without taking a gift.

BABUSHKA TURNS BACK **(⊙ Track 10 / 23)**

[The music plays quietly under the Narrator's lines. Scenery may be changed. ANGELS move aside. Nativity scene is set. JOSEPH needs his bottle & glass. Once all is set, MARY stands.]

SCENE 4 In The Stable

NARRATOR 1 — But suddenly Babushka heard someone calling her name!

MARY — Babushka! Come back!

[BABUSHKA turns round.]

NARRATOR 2 — Babushka wondered who it was, and how this person knew her name! She saw a woman standing outside a stable. The woman called her again.

MARY — Babushka! I'm Mary. It's my baby you've come to see!

BABUSHKA — But I have nothing to give your baby!

MARY	Oh yes you have! Come and see!
NARRATOR 1	Babushka was puzzled. She went into the stable with Mary and was shocked at how dirty it was.
BABUSHKA	*(gasps, pointing)* Look at all those dirty animals!
DONKEY	*(crossly)* Ee-orrh! She's so rude! *(very crossly)* Ee-orrh!
	[BABUSHKA walks around the stable area, peering at the animals, hands on hips.]
ALL	Shush, Donkey! Now you're being rude!
BABUSHKA	*(shaking her head)* Tut, tut, tut! Just look at those horrible cobwebs! I'd better tidy up!
NARRATOR 2	She was about to get a duster out of her basket, but an amazing sight met her eyes.
	[MARY picks up baby Jesus so that all can see. As the NARRATOR speaks, BABUSHKA goes to MARY.]
NARRATOR 1	There was the baby, wrapped in a warm shawl.
BABUSHKA	*(pointing, puzzled)* But that's the shawl I gave to the shepherd boy!
	[BABUSHKA shakes her head and walks to manger.]
NARRATOR 2	Then Babushka noticed a little doll lying in the manger.
	[JOSEPH begins to mime pouring his cordial.]
BABUSHKA	*(pointing, amazed)* But that's the doll I gave the little girl!
NARRATOR 1	Joseph was pouring a glass of cordial. Babushka couldn't believe her eyes.
BABUSHKA	*(pointing, astonished)* But that's the cordial I gave to the old woman!
NARRATOR 2	Mary told Babushka something very strange and amazing.
MARY	Everything you gave with love, you gave to my son.
	[BABUSHKA matches actions to NARRATOR's words.]
NARRATOR 1	Babushka shrugged. She didn't understand. Shaking her head, she turned away and took a duster out of her basket. She was about to start cleaning when Mary stopped her.
	[MARY lifts the baby and holds him out to BABUSHKA.]
MARY	Babushka, wouldn't you like to hold my baby?
	[BABUSHKA smiles a big smile, and takes the baby.]
NARRATOR 2	Babushka held the baby and looked at him. She couldn't help noticing that his eyes were amazing. They were as deep as the deep starry night.

EVERYTHING YOU GIVE (⊙ Track 11 / 24)

Mary WHEN HE SMILES,
WHAT A GENTLE SMILE,
FULL OF PURE LOVE.
THIS CHILD,
WHAT A GENTLE CHILD,
FULL OF PURE LOVE.

EVERYTHING YOU GIVE WITH LOVE
YOU GIVE TO HIM.
All AMAZING!
Mary EVERYTHING YOU SAY WITH LOVE
YOU SAY TO HIM.
All AMAZING!
Mary EVERYTHING YOU DO WITH LOVE
YOU DO FOR HIM,
'COS HE IS LOVE.

[DONKEY & SHEEP move next to BABUSHKA.]

All WHEN HE SMILES,
WHAT A GENTLE SMILE,
FULL OF PURE LOVE.
THIS CHILD,
WHAT A GENTLE CHILD,
FULL OF PURE LOVE.

EVERYTHING YOU GIVE WITH LOVE
YOU GIVE TO HIM.
AMAZING!
EVERYTHING YOU SAY WITH LOVE
YOU SAY TO HIM.
AMAZING!
EVERYTHING YOU DO WITH LOVE
YOU DO FOR HIM,
'COS HE IS LOVE.
YES HE IS LOVE.

NARRATOR 1 A strange feeling had crept over Babushka. This feeling was so good that she forgot all about tidying up.

NARRATOR 2 The donkey nuzzled up close to her, but instead of complaining about him being dirty, she stroked his nose.

DONKEY *(sweetly, leaning his head on her shoulder)* Hello, Babushka!

BABUSHKA *(affectionately hugging him)* Hello, lovely donkey!

NARRATORS What had happened to Babushka?

ALL What's happened to you, Babushka?

BABUSHKA I don't know!

NARRATORS Babushka didn't know, but the angels did!

ANGELS	She's found peace!
NARRATOR 2	Peace had filled the empty place in Babushka's heart.

<u>BABUSHKA</u> (Full Heart) **(⊙ Track 12 / 25)**

BABUSHKA. BABUSHKA.
SHE FILLED THE EMPTY PLACE IN HER HEART.

HAPPY, HAPPY,
HAPPY ALL DAY LONG.
NOW BABUSHKA'S HEART IS FULL,
HAPPY ALL DAY LONG.

JESUS TAUGHT HER,
TAUGHT HER HOW TO LOVE.
NOW BABUSHKA'S HEART IS FULL:

(spoken) Hey, Babushka!

JESUS TAUGHT YOU LOVE.

BABUSHKA. BABUSHKA.
SHE FILLED THE EMPTY PLACE IN HER HEART.
FILLED THE EMPTY PLACE IN HER HEART.
(shouted) HOI!

[KINGS & CAMELS move into position.]

NARRATOR 1	Just as Babushka handed baby Jesus back to Mary, there was a knock at the door. *[Knocking sound.]* It was the three kings and their camels.
JOSEPH	Come in!
KINGS	But our feet are dirty!
JOSEPH	*(pointing at the floor)* So is the floor! This isn't a palace, you know.
MARY	You can come in just as you are.
KING 1	*(In a posh voice)* I say, you're very kind.
KINGS 2 & 3	But what about our camels?
JOSEPH	*(opening arms wide)* It's a stable! They can come in too.
CAMELS/KINGS	Thank you!
NARRATOR 2	The kings and camels went into the stable. Babushka was ashamed that she'd been so rude when they came to her door.
BABUSHKA	I'm sorry. I was very rude when you came to my door.
KING 2	That's ok Babushka. Actually you did us a favour.

KING 3	We got lots of exercise chasing after the camels!
KING 1	*(in a posh voice)* I say, everyone! Just look at our leg muscles!
	[KINGS exhibit their calves proudly!]
ALL	Very impressive!
CAMELS	*(coughing politely)* Ahem! Ahem! Have you forgotten why we came?
CAMEL 1	Or did you just want to show off your muscles?
KINGS	Of course not!
KING 1	*(posh, wagging his finger)* No, no, no, no! *(hands on his hips)* We didn't come to show off our muscles!
KINGS 2 & 3	We've brought gifts for the baby.
	[KINGS take their gifts from the camels.]
KING 1	*(presents gift and kneels)* I've brought gold.
KING 2	*(presents gift and kneels)* I've brought frankincense.
KING 3	*(presents gift and kneels)* And I've brought myrrh.
NARRATOR 1	As the kings knelt down by the manger they couldn't help noticing this was a very special baby. Babushka was watching the kings. She could see they had been filled with peace, just like her.
KINGS	This isn't a palace, but *(pointing)* this baby is a king.
NARRATOR 2	All of a sudden, happiness bubbled up inside Babushka.
BABUSHKA	*(dancing about)* Oh, goodness me! My feet won't stay still! They want to dance!
ALL	Dance, Babushka!
KINGS	*(dancing about)* Oh! Our feet want to dance too!
ALL	Dance with Babushka!
	[KINGS take turns to link arms with BABUSHKA and they dance about as the next line is given.]
NARRATOR 1 & 2	Babushka's life had changed. She would never feel empty again!
	[Move children into place for finale while replaying track 25, fade out when all in position. During the song, children should all be moving about in some way, even if it is on the spot. A Cossack dance effect can be achieved by having some children sitting on a low bench or staging block and doing L / R kicks with arms - folded across chest in 'Cossack' style. A group could be seated doing this during the song, while others perform standing.]

MY FEET WANT TO DANCE (⊙ Track 13 / 26)

MY FEET WANT TO DANCE *(stamp, stamp)*
FROM NIGHT TIME 'TIL MORNING.
MY FEET WANT TO DANCE *(stamp, stamp)*
THE WHOLE DAY LONG.
MY HANDS WANT TO CLAP *(clap, clap)*
FROM NIGHT TIME 'TIL MORNING.
MY HANDS WANT TO CLAP *(clap, clap)*
THE WHOLE DAY LONG.

Clap in time with the music. →

'COS I'M FEELING FULL OF JOY,
FEELING FULL OF LIFE.
WANT TO SHARE IT WITH THE REST OF THE WORLD.
YES, I'M FEELING FULL OF JOY,
FEELING FULL OF LIFE.
WANT TO SHARE IT WITH THE REST OF THE WORLD.
YES I DO!

MY HEART WANTS TO SING *(stretch arm out)*
FROM NIGHT TIME 'TIL MORNING.
MY HEART WANTS TO SING *(stretch arm out)*
THE WHOLE DAY LONG.
MY ARMS WANT TO WAVE *(wave whole arm)*
FROM NIGHT TIME 'TIL MORNING.
MY ARMS WANT TO WAVE *(wave whole arm)*
THE WHOLE DAY LONG.

Clap in time with the music. →

'COS I'M FEELING FULL OF JOY,
FEELING FULL OF LIFE.
WANT TO SHARE IT WITH THE REST OF THE WORLD.
YES, I'M FEELING FULL OF JOY,
FEELING FULL OF LIFE.
WANT TO SHARE IT WITH THE REST OF THE WORLD.
GONNA SHARE IT WITH THE REST OF THE WORLD!
(shouted, while punching the air) HOI!

Tel: +44 (0) 1323 764334
Fax: +44 (0) 1323 767145
Website: www.starshine.co.uk
e-mail: info@starshine.co.uk

Matrioshka
(Babushka)
Nesting Dolls

One of the most famous souvenirs sold in Russsia is the Matrioshka nest doll, often wrongly called a Babushka doll. Matrioshka dolls are made of wood and have smaller dolls stacked within the bigger ones.

The word 'babushka' in Russian means 'grandmother'. You can see why people call the dolls Babushka dolls, as they are designed so that a whole set will fit one inside another, like generations of children. The biggest doll seems like the great grandmother of the smaller ones!

The word 'Matrioshka' comes from the name Matrena, which was the most popular girl's name in Russia form many centuries. The word is a translation from the old Slav language and means 'mother'. The dolls are often seen as a symbol of fertility.

Usually matrioshkas have anything from two to twenty-four dolls inside each other, but occasionally there have been nesting dolls with many more that that inside - the most being an unbelieveable <u>sixty</u>!

The first Russian nesting doll (Matrioshka) was made in 1890 just outside Moscow in a place called Sergiev Posad, a colourful Russian town with a large monastry. In front of the monastry was a huge market place which would usually be crowded with all kinds of people - traders, pilgrims, craftsmen, villagers - all going about their business.

The first nesting dolls made were designed to portray the colourful life of Sergiev Posad, and were painted to show young girls in Russian costume, maybe carrying scythes or bunches of flowers, or dressed in winter short fur coats and scarves. Sometimes dolls were even painted to show bearded men or old peasant women.

Track 1 / 14

Russian Villagers' Dance

Music & Lyrics by Ruth Kenward
Edited by Simon Walters

Steadily (♩ = 140)

Dm
A
Dm
C
F
A
Dm
Ly - ly - ly - ly - ly.
Ly - ly - ly - ly-
A
ly.
Ly - ly - ly - ly - ly.

A
Dm
Ly - ly___ ly ly - ly - ly - ly ly.
Hoi!
Much slower ♩ = 70
A
Dm
A
poco a poco accel...
Dm
A
Dm

Faster ♩ = 170
C
F
A
Ly-ly-ly-ly - ly.
Dm
A
Ly-ly-ly-ly - ly.
Ly-ly-ly-ly - ly.
A
Dm
Ly - ly ly ly - ly - ly - ly ly.
Hoi!

Track 2 / 15

You'll Never Find A Mouse

Music & Lyrics by Ruth Kenward
Edited by Simon Walters

Briskly (♩ = 120)

spi-der to be seen. Far too clean for a spi-der to be seen.
Bye, bye, spi-der Bye, bye, spi-der
You'll ne-ver find a fly buzz-ing, buzz-ing by. It's
far too clean for a fly to be seen. Far too clean for a
fly to be seen. Bye, bye, fly! Bye, bye, fly!
rit.
Slower (♩ = 90)
You'll ne-ver find (clap, clap) a speck of dust. (clap, clap) Ba-
rall.
bush-ka cleans (clap, clap) from dawn 'til dusk!

Track 3 / 16

Babushka

(Empty Heart)

Music & Lyrics by Ruth Kenward
Arranged by Simon Walters

Sadly (♩ = 80)

Busily (♩ = 120)
Cm
mf
Sweep - ing, sweep - ing,
Dust - ing, dust - ing,
Wash - ing, wash - ing,
B♭
G7
sweep - ing all day long. She's no time to
dust - ing all day long.
wash - ing all day long.
Cm
stop and think, sweep - ing all day long.
dust - ing all day long.
wash - ing all day long.

Cm
Bu - sy, bu - sy,
B♭
G7
bu - sy all day long. She's no time to stop and think:
N.C.
G7
(spoken)
Stop, Ba-bush-ka! It's al - rea - dy
rit.

Sadly (♩ = 80)

Cm
clean! Ba- bush-ka, Ba-
mp
B♭ Gm Cm
bush- ka, she hides an emp-ty place in her heart.
rall.

Track 4 / 17

Wipe Your Feet

Music & Lyrics by Ruth Kenward
Additional Lyrics by Maggie Hughes
Edited by Simon Walters

Grandly (♩ = 120)

Busily (♩= 150)
D
G
(spoken)
while? Please? BABUSHKA: Wipe your feet! Wipe your
f
Em7
C/D
1.
G
feet! Wipe your nas - ty, dir - ty feet! ALL: Wipe your
1st Tempo (♩ = 120)
2.
G
D
G
Am7
(spoken)
KINGS: (spoken ad lib)
feet! Wipe your feet! Huh! She ought to be more po-
rall.
3

G/B G/D C D C G C/D
lite! We're kings! 2. CAMELS: We are the ca-mel
tr
mf
G D/F♯ Em
train. Car-ry-ing kings is a pain.
mf
mf mf
mf
C D
We're ta-king gifts to a child. May we rest for a

D
while? May we rest for a while? (spoken) Please?
Busily (♩ = 150)
G
Em7
BABUSHKA: Wipe your hooves! Wipe your hooves! Wipe your
f
C/D
1. G
2. G
nas-ty, dir-ty hooves! ALL: Wipe your hooves! (spoken) Wipe your hooves!
rit.

Track 5 / 18

There's A Stable

Music & Lyrics by Ruth Kenward
Edited by Simon Walters

Gently (♩ = 120)

E/G♯ E7 A
dus - ty, gloo - my and cold. But to -
dus - ty, gloo - my and cold. But to -
o - pen, they just can't sleep. 'Cos to -
D C♯ C♯/F
night that tat - ty sta - ble is bla - zing with
night that tat - ty sta - ble is bla - zing with
night that tat - ty sta - ble is bla - zing with
F♯m D E7sus4 E7
light, 'cos a ba - by's been born to -
light, 'cos a ba - by's been born to -
light, 'cos a ba - by's been born to -

1.2.
A
Esus4
E
3.A
night.
2. ALL There's a
night.
3. ANGEL In the
night.
F♯m
D
E7sus4
E7
A
Yes, a ba - by's been born to - night.
mp
rall.

Track 6 / 19

Babushka Packs Her Basket

Music & Lyrics by Ruth Kenward
Edited by Simon Walters

Steadily (♩ = 140)

Repeat if necessary.

Track 7 / 20

To Bethlehem

Music & Lyrics by Ruth Kenward
Edited by Simon Walters

Steadily (𝅗𝅥 = 95)

E♭maj7
F
I shall find the ba - by.
she will find the ba - by.
E♭
F
she will find the ba - by.
rall.

To Bethlehem

(Reprise)

Music & Lyrics by Ruth Kenward

Edited by Simon Walters

Steadily (𝅗𝅥 = 95)

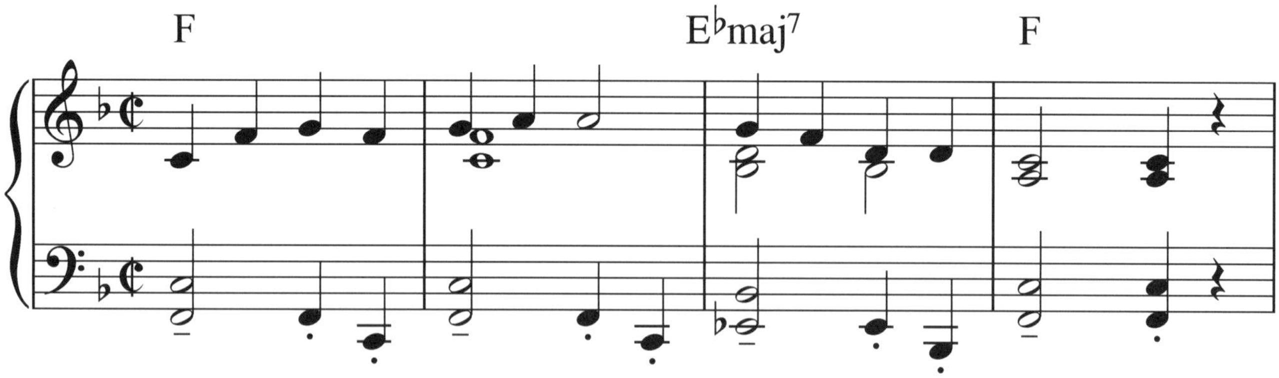

E♭maj7
F
she will find the ba - by.
E♭
F
she will find the ba - by.
rall.

Track 10 / 23

Babushka Turns Back

Music by Ruth Kenward
Edited by Simon Walters

Softly (𝅗𝅥 = 65)

Everything You Give

Music & Lyrics by Ruth Kenward
Edited by Simon Walters

Gently (𝅗𝅥 = 65)

D/C♯ G G/A D
gen - tle child, full of pure love.
Bm A/C♯ Em7
MARY: Ev - 'ry - thing you give with love you give to him. ALL: A -
ALL: Ev - 'ry - thing you give with love you give to him. A -
mf
G A Bm A/C♯
ma - zing! MARY: Ev - 'ry - thing you say with love you
ma - zing! Ev - 'ry - thing you say with love you

G/B G A Bm
say to him. ALL: A - ma - zing! MARY: Ev - 'ry - thing you
say to him. A - ma - zing! Ev - 'ry - thing you
A/C♯ Em7 G A
do with love you do for him, 'cos he is
do with love you do for him, 'cos he is
1. D D/C♯ G G/A
love. 2. ALL: When he
mp

2. Bm
D/A
G♯m-5
love.
Yes,
G/A
A
D
he
is
love.
rit.

Track 12 / 25

Babushka

(Full Heart)

Music & Lyrics by Ruth Kenward
Edited by Simon Walters

Happily (♩ = 90)

Energetically (♩ = 120)
Cm
Hap - py, hap - py,
f
B♭
G7
hap - py all day long. Now Ba - bush - ka's
Cm
heart is full, hap - py all day long.

Cm
Je - sus taught her, taught her how to
G7
love. Now Ba - bush - ka's heart is full.
N.C.
G7
(spoken) Hey, Ba-bush-ka!
Je - sus taught you

Cm
love! Ba - bush - ka, Ba - bush - ka,
poco a poco cresc. e accel.
B♭ Gm A♭
she filled the emp - ty place in her heart.
G7 Cm
Filled the emp - ty place in her heart
Hoi!

My Feet Want To Dance

Music & Lyrics by Ruth Kenward
Edited by Simon Walters

Exuberant! (♩ = 190)

F G7 C
dance (stamp, stamp) from night time_ 'til mor - ning. My
clap (clap, clap)
F 1. G C
feet want_ to dance (stamp, stamp) the whole day_ long.
hands want_ to clap (clap, clap)
N.C. 2. G C N.C.
My whole day_ long. 'cos I'm fee - ling

F F/G C F F/G C
full of joy feel-ing full of life want to
f
F C/E Dm7 C G
1. N.C.
share it with the rest of the world (clap, clap, clap, clap) Yes, I'm fee-ling
2.
A
clap) Yes I do, (clap, clap, clap, clap) My

D
G
A7
heart wants to sing from night time_ 'til
arms want_ to wave
mf
D
G
mor - ning. My heart wants to sing the
arms want to wave
1. A
D
N.C.
whole day long. My

2.
A D N.C. G G/A D
whole day long. 'cos I'm fee - ling full of joy
f
G G/A D G D/F♯
feel - ing full of life want to share it with the
1.
Em7 D A N.C.
rest of the world (clap, clap, clap, clap) Yes, I'm fee - ling

2.
G D/F♯ G A D
clap) Gon - na share it with the rest of the world
(clap, clap, clap, clap) HOI!

Babushka
(Narrative Version)

<u>SCENE 1 Outside Babushka's House</u>

[Enter VILLAGERS, meeting and greeting in a dance.]

<u>RUSSIAN VILLAGERS DANCE</u> (⊙ Track 1 / 14)

<u>SCENE 2 Inside Babushka's House</u>

NARRATOR 1 — Long ago, in a Russian village, there lived a little old woman called Babushka. She was as round and kindly as a warm plum pudding.

[Enter BABUSHKA, sweeping and dusting.]

NARRATOR 2 — While everyone else was dancing, she would sweep, dust and polish from sunrise to starshine.

NARRATOR 3 — Her house was the cleanest in the whole of Russia.

[MOUSE, SPIDER & FLY enter (or two of each) for each appropriate verse, at the end of which BABUSHKA chases them off with her broom.]

<u>YOU'LL NEVER FIND A MOUSE</u> (⊙ Track 2 / 15)

[BABUSHKA keeps cleaning, her back to SPIDER, MOUSE & FLY.]

NARRATOR 4 — Babushka hated flies, mice and spiders. She thought they were horrible and dirty, so she chased them away.

[BABUSHKA notices FLY, MOUSE & SPIDER again and chases them away with her broom, then moves around miming cleaning activities. This continues throughout the following song, making her actions match the words. The CHORUS can mime the same activities.]

NARRATOR 1 — Babushka kept busy all the time because she had an empty place in her heart.

NARRATOR 2 — Poor Babushka. She was busy but she wasn't happy.

<u>BABUSHKA</u> (Empty Heart) (⊙ Track 3 / 16)

[BABUSHKA sits in her chair and polishes candlesticks through the following narration.]

NARRATOR 3 — Poor Babushka had no friends. She was very lonely. All she did was clean her house.

NARRATOR 4 — One evening a bright new star shone through Babushka's window.

[STAR moves into position.]

NARRATOR 1 — She was polishing her candlesticks, when something made her look at the window. Look at the star, Babushka!

[BABUSHKA looks towards the window.]

ALL — Look, Babushka!

NARRATOR 2 — But she didn't notice the star. She was too busy noticing a dirty mark on the window pane.

[BABUSHKA takes a cloth, goes to the window and cleans it.]

NARRATOR 3 — While she was busy cleaning the window, the star disappeared behind a cloud.

[STAR moves out of sight. ANGEL moves into view. BABUSHKA peers out of the window.]

NARRATOR 4 — When the window was clean she could see out, but it was too late for Babushka to see the star.

NARRATOR 1 — But she saw something else instead – an angel! And the angel told Babushka he had good news.

ALL — Listen to the news, Babushka!

NARRATOR 2 — But Babushka wasn't interested. She only cared about keeping her floor clean. She told the angel he'd have to wipe his feet if he wanted to come in!

[ANGEL looks very sad, wings droop, head hangs.]

That made the angel very sad, and he flew away.

ALL — Ahh.... poor angel.

[Exit ANGEL, flapping wings. BABUSHKA goes back to her chair and polishes. KINGS approach the door.]

NARRATOR 3 — Babushka wondered what the angel's news might have been. But it was too late to find out.

NARRATOR 4 — Soon there was a knock at the door. Babushka wondered who it could be.

[Knocking sound. BABUSHKA mimes opening a door. Enter KINGS, to stand centrally and sing. BABUSHKA stands with her arms folded looking suspicious.]

WIPE YOUR FEET (⊙ Track 4 / 17)

NARRATOR 1 — Babushka shooed the camels away, telling them they were too dirty to come in.

[BABUSHKA shoos CAMELS, who run away.]

The camels were scared of Babushka and they ran away very quickly!

NARRATOR 2 — The Kings were alarmed! They didn't want to lose their camels, so they ran after them.

[KINGS run off. BABUSHKA sits on her chair.]

Babushka was tired after all that fuss, so she sat down for a rest.

NARRATOR 3 — She thought about the kings and the camels, and the long journey they must have had.

[BABUSHKA tuts and shakes her head as if thinking about their long journey.]

She felt sorry for the kings and the camels, but she couldn't have coped with all those dirty feet and hooves.

NARRATOR 4 — Babushka yawned, and very soon she fell asleep.

[BABUSHKA yawns, stretches, then settles to sleep.]

While she was sleeping the angel came back and sang a song about a baby being born.

[If time for movement onto stage is needed, use the backing to play ANGELS, DONKEYS & SHEEP on, fading out when ready and re-starting the track.]

THERE'S A STABLE (⊙ Track 5 / 18)

[STAR moves into position during last line of song.]

NARRATOR 1 — As the angel finished singing, the star peeped out from behind the cloud and shone in through the window. It woke Babushka up.

[BABUSHKA yawns and stretches.]

NARRATOR 2 — She remembered what she'd heard while she was sleeping. It was a story about a brand new baby in a dirty old stable!

[BABUSHKA puts her hands on hips and looks first disgusted, then concerned.

NARRATOR 3 — 'How disgusting!' she thought. She knew she had to do something to help this little baby. She felt so sorry for him, born in a scruffy stable.

[BABUSHKA starts packing her basket, and keeps miming getting ready to go throughout the music.]

BABUSHKA PACKS HER BASKET (⊙ Track 6 / 19)

NARRATOR 4 — *(speaking over the incidental music)* Babushka packed a basket with a little toy doll, a warm shawl and a bottle of ginger cordial for the grown-ups. She also packed some cleaning equipment.

[Chair is removed. Scenery may be changed, and ANGELS begin to spread out at the back of the performing area.]

SCENE 3 Babushka's Journey

NARRATOR 1 — Outside the house the sky grew very bright as lots of angels crowded around. They watched over Babushka as she set out on her journey, but she didn't notice them.

[BABUSHKA stands with her basket over her arm to sing the first verse, then sets off walking around as if on a journey, while the ANGELS & all other performers sing verse 2. A few ANGELS may follow BABUSHKA.]

TO BETHLEHEM (⊙ Track 7 / 20)

[MOTHER enters, holding the hand of CHILD, who is crying loudly. CHILD gets out enormously big, long hankie from pocket, and blows nose very loudly.]

NARRATOR 2 — On her journey she met a woman whose little girl was crying. Babushka wondered why she was so unhappy, and asked what was the matter.

NARRATOR 3 — The mother told her that they had been running to see a new king and the little girl had dropped her dolly.

[CHILD wails very sadly, in an obviously exaggerated way until the audience laugh. BABUSHKA gets out the doll during the laughter and narration.]

NARRATOR 4 — Babushka took the toy doll out of her basket and jiggled it to make it dance. The little girl stopped crying and pointed at the doll with a big smile.

NARRATOR 1 — The mother was very grateful to Babushka, and they went on their way.

NARRATOR 2 — Babushka waved goodbye, and then continued on her journey, thinking it was interesting that they were going to see a new King.

[BABUSHKA walks around as if on a journey. A few ANGELS may follow her.]

TO BETHLEHEM (reprise) (⊙ Track 8 / 21)

[OLD WOMAN enters, bent over, hobbling with a stick and clutching her back.]

NARRATOR 3 Next she met an old woman who was going to see a new baby, she was tired and thirsty, and her legs ached so much that she could only go very slowly.

NARRATOR 4 Babushka took the bottle of cordial out of her basket and gave it to the old woman.

NARRATOR 1 The old woman took a big drink and all of a sudden she stood up straight with a big smile and then she skipped and jumped! She felt ten years younger!

NARRATOR 2 Now it would be an easy journey to see the new baby! The old woman went on her way.

[OLD WOMAN exits, waving, then goes to join nativity group. BABUSHKA waves her off. OLD WOMAN must remember to give the bottle of cordial to JOSEPH.]

NARRATOR 3 Babushka waved goodbye, and then continued on her journey, thinking it was interesting that the old woman was going to see a new baby. She was going to see a new baby too!

[BABUSHKA walks around as if on a journey. A few ANGELS may follow her.]

TO BETHLEHEM (reprise) (⊙ Track 9 / 22)

[SHEPHERD BOY enters carrying a lamb, shivering and rubbing his arms.]

NARRATOR 4 Next she met a shepherd boy. He was carrying a lamb, and he was shivering with cold. He couldn't carry the lamb much further.

[BABUSHKA gets out the shawl during the narration.]

NARRATOR 1 Babushka took the warm shawl out of her basket. She put the basket down, and wrapped the shawl around the shepherd boy's shoulders.

NARRATOR 2 The shepherd boy stopped shivering and smiled at Babushka. Now he would be able to catch up the other shepherds on their journey to see the new baby king!

[SHEPHERD BOY exits, waving, then goes to join nativity group. BABUSHKA waves him off. SHEPHERD BOY must put the shawl around the Jesus doll.]

NARRATOR 3 Babushka waved goodbye, and then continued on her journey, thinking it was interesting that the shepherds were going to see a new baby king.

NARRATOR 4 Then Babushka realised something awful.

[BABUSHKA picks up her basket and gives a gasp.]

She'd given away all the presents she had packed to give to the new baby.

NARRATOR 1	Sadly, she turned back towards home. She didn't want to go and see a new baby without taking a gift.

BABUSHKA TURNS BACK **(⊙ Track 10 / 23)**

[The music plays quietly under the Narrator's lines. Scenery may be changed. ANGELS move aside. Nativity scene is set. JOSEPH needs his bottle and glass. Once all is set, MARY stands.]

SCENE 4 In The Stable

NARRATOR 2 — But suddenly Babushka heard someone calling her name!

[BABUSHKA turns round. MARY beckons.]

She wondered who it was, and how this person knew her name!

NARRATOR 3 — She saw a woman standing outside a stable. It was Mary! Mary called her again, telling her to come inside the stable to see her baby.

[BABUSHKA shakes her head and looks worried, and shows her empty basket.]

NARRATOR 4 — When Babushka said her she had nothing to give to the baby, Mary told her that she did have something to give!

NARRATOR 1 — Babushka didn't understand. She was puzzled, but she went into the stable with Mary to see.

NARRATOR 2 — She was very shocked at how dirty it was.

[BABUSHKA points at the cobwebs and animals, pulling a face that says 'dirty!' The animals look offended.]

She pulled out a duster, ready to clean the stable, but then an amazing sight met her eyes.

[MARY picks up baby Jesus so that all can see. As the NARRATOR speaks, BABUSHKA goes to MARY, pointing in amazement.]

NARRATOR 3 — There was the baby, wrapped in a warm shawl, the same shawl that she had given to the shepherd boy!

[BABUSHKA shakes her head and walks to manger, then points again, amazed.]

NARRATOR 4 — Then Babushka noticed a little doll lying in the manger.

[JOSEPH begins to mime pouring his cordial]

It was the same doll that she had give to the little girl!

NARRATOR 1 — Joseph was pouring a glass of cordial. Babushka couldn't believe her eyes. It was the same cordial she had given to the old woman!

[BABUSHKA and MARY mime to the NARRATORS' words.]

NARRATOR 2	Then Mary told her something very strange and amazing. She said that everything Babushka had given away with love had been a gift to baby Jesus.
NARRATOR 3	A gift to baby Jesus? How could that be? She had never even seen the baby. Babushka shrugged. She didn't understand.
NARRATOR 4	Shaking her head, she turned away and took a duster out of her basket. She was about to start cleaning when Mary gave her the baby to hold.
	[MARY lifts the baby and holds him out to BABUSHKA, who smiles a big smile, and takes the baby]
NARRATOR 1	Babushka held the baby and looked at him. She couldn't help noticing that his eyes were amazing. They were as deep as the deep starry night.

EVERYTHING YOU GIVE **(⊙ Track 11 / 24)**

NARRATOR 2	A strange feeling had crept over Babushka. This feeling was so good that she forgot all about tidying up.
NARRATOR 3	The donkey nuzzled up close to her, but instead of complaining about him being dirty, she stroked his nose.
NARRATORS	What had happened to Babushka?
ALL	What's happened to you, Babushka?
	[BABUSHKA shrugs.]
NARRATORS	Babushka didn't know, but the angels did!
NARRATOR 4	Peace had filled the empty place in Babushka's heart.

BABUSHKA (Full Heart) **(⊙ Track 12 / 25)**

[KINGS & CAMELS move into position.]

NARRATOR 4	Just as Babushka handed baby Jesus back to Mary, there was a knock at the door.
	[Knocking sound]
	It was the three kings and their camels.
NARRATOR 1	They wanted to come in but they were worried about their dirty feet. Dirty feet don't matter in a stable, so Mary and Joseph invited them in.
NARRATOR 2	Babushka was ashamed that she'd been so rude when they came to her door. She apologised, but they told her not to worry.
NARRATOR 3	They said she had done them a favour, because they got lots of exercise chasing after the camels!
	[KINGS exhibit their leg muscles proudly.]

ALL	Look at those leg muscles!
NARRATOR 4	The camels reminded the Kings that they needed to give their gifts to the baby.
	[KINGS take their gifts from the camels and kneel at the manger. JOSEPH receives their gifts.]
	The first king gave gold. The second king gave frankincense. And the third king gave myrrh.
NARRATOR 1	As the kings knelt down by the manger they couldn't help noticing that this was a very special baby.
NARRATOR 2	Babushka was watching the kings. She could see they had been filled with peace, just like her.
NARRATOR 3	All of a sudden, happiness bubbled up inside Babushka. She felt so full of joy that she wanted to dance!
ALL	Dance, Babushka!
	[BABUSHKA dances about.]
NARRATOR 4	The kings wanted to dance too!
ALL	Dance with Babushka!
	[KINGS take turns to link arms with Babushka and they dance about as the next line is given.]
NARRATORS	Babushka's life had changed. She would never feel empty again!
	[Move children into place for finale with some of the backing track, fade out when all in position. During the song, children should all be moving in some way, even if it is on the spot. A Cossack dance effect can be achieved by having some children sitting on a low bench or staging block and doing L / R kicks with 'Cossack' arms - folded across chest. A group could be seated doing this during the song, while others perform standing.]

MY FEET WANT TO DANCE **(⊙ Track 13 / 26)**

Tel: +44 (0) 1323 764334
Fax: +44 (0) 1323 767145
Website: www.starshine.co.uk
e-mail: info@starshine.co.uk

PERFORMING RIGHTS FOR THE SHOW

LICENCE APPLICATION

If you are planning to stage this musical, or to record the performance and/or songs, you will need to apply for a Licence. 'Block' licences which your school/group may have do not cover performances of musicals, licences for which are only available directly from publishers. To perform any musical without a specific licence to do so from its publisher is illegal.

Revenue raised from Performing Licences is the main source of income for writers. Licence charges vary according to publishers and performing circumstances, but our licence fees are very reasonable and safeguard you from prosecution. A quotation for your proposed production may be obtained from Starshine Music by phone / e-mail / website. Alternatively, you may complete the form below, and post or fax it to:

Starshine Music, Brown Cottage, Glynleigh Rd, Hankham, E. Sussex, England. BN24 5BJ.
Tel: +44 (0)1323 764334 Fax: +44 (0)1323 767145
Website: www.starshine.co.uk

Please give me a price quotation ☐ **Please process this application** ☐

APPLICATION TO PERFORM:

'Babushka' by Ruth Kenward

Name of school / group ....

Date(s) of production ....

Venue ....

Number of performances ....

Expected audience size per performance ....

Will admissions be charged (& if so, at what rate)? ....

Name of producer ....

Address of school / group..

....

Postcode..

Daytime telephone number .... Fax: ....

e-mail address ....

If you are intending to record the show, or any part of it, please estimate the number of copies you will be producing. (Include an approximate figure to cover parents making full-length video recordings, as well as any 'official' school recordings.)

DVD/VIDEO RECORDING	1*	2-25	26-50	51-75	76-100	100+
SOUND RECORDING	1*	2-25	26-50	51-75	76-100	100+

*for school/organisation archive purposes

Index of Musical Items